Gloria Morgan has been writing since she was ten. She grew up in London but now lives half way up the M1, on the left. Her favourite colour is red and her favourite day is Thursday. She's had various jobs in offices, colleges, hospitals and photographic studios while the stories and plays have just kept coming. She enjoys travelling and some of the interesting people and places she's seen have found their way into her books. Best of all, Gloria likes to write for young readers. She spends most of her time at her computer bashing away at her latest manuscript. When she drags herself away from the screen she enjoys pottering in her garden and going for long walks, preferably with a dog. To find out what she's working on now visit her website: www.callie-cobooks.co.uk

By the same author:

Kinmers Lea
The Ducking Stool
Dream Me Home

For slightly younger readers:

Shan and the Tree
Shan and the Snow
Shan and the Pond

Cassie

The Story of a Rescue Dog

The first 6 months

Gloria Morgan

Copyright © Gloria Morgan 2011

The right of Gloria Morgan to be identified as the Author of the Work has been asserted by her in accordance with the Copyright, Designs and Patents Act 1988.

This publication may only be reproduced, stored, or transmitted, in any form, or by any means, with prior permission in writing from the author.

A CIP catalogue record for this title is available from the British Library

ISBN
978-184426-977-8

First published in 2011
by
Callie-Co Books, Nottingham

www.callie-cobooks.co.uk

Printed and bound by print-on-demand-worldwide.com

Contents

Chapter 1	Introductions
Chapter 2	Early Days
Chapter 3	All Change
Chapter 4	Rescue
Chapter 5	New Home
Chapter 6	Walkies
Chapter 7	Friends
Chapter 8	Training
Chapter 9	Bad Dog
Chapter 10	Big Sisters
Chapter 11	Proud Day
Chapter 12	The Future

Author's Note

Everything in the story after Cassie came into my home six months ago has been written from my experience of living with her and loving her to bits.

My thanks to our obedience trainer who has given me many wise insights into collie behaviour in general and Cassie's in particular; also to other dog owners who have offered helpful comments based on their own experience of adopting a rescue dog.

The things I have included about Cassie's life before she came to me have been pieced together from several sources – information given to me by the rescue when I fetched her; comments made by my vet when he first examined her; and research I have done about the various behaviours she has displayed.

I confess the details of her very early life are invented as there is no one to tell me what they were really like. However, I don't think her puppy days would have been very different from what I have described.

I'm so proud of this dog and what she has achieved since she moved in with me.

She is my shadow – a sweet-natured, bright-eyed, affectionate companion who lights up my life.

In the end, I have left it to Cassie to tell her own story.

Gloria Morgan
January 2011

Cassie

The Story of a Rescue Dog

The first 6 months

Chapter 1 – Introductions

Hello – my name is Cassie. I'm a Border collie and I was rescued. I'm going to tell you all about myself, how I started life and the many different things that have happened to me over the years.

First of all I'm going to make a list of all the things I have that belong to me. I've got:

    a dinner bowl
    a water bowl
    a collar and lead
    a towel
    a brush
    a basket
    a little toy lion
    a ball
    a jar of biscuits in the kitchen
    a big cage in the sitting room
    a smaller cage in the car
    a kennel on the yard

With a huge list like that you must think I am loved and adored by an owner who gives me everything a dog could possibly want. You would be right, of course, except it wasn't always like that.

Before I came to live here I had nothing – absolutely nothing. I didn't even know dogs could have things that belonged to them. Let me tell you about my life and the huge changes I have seen.

Chapter 2 – Early Days

I was born about seven years ago on a farm deep in the countryside. I was the only female in a litter of four puppies. My parents were sheepdogs. They were called Scout and Tammy. They went out into the fields every day with the farmer to tend the sheep. They were very clever dogs. You may have seen sheepdogs on TV taking part in competitions.

Herding is a natural instinct in collies but still there is a lot to learn. The dogs don't decide for themselves where to run. The farmer gives them instructions about what to do, either by calling out to them or whistling.

The sheep need to be moved regularly from one field to another where there is fresh grass. At certain times the sheep have to be fetched from the fields into the farm-yard. Sometimes the farmer needs the dogs to separate one sheep from the rest of the flock.

The dogs have to learn what all the farmer's instructions mean and then they have to be brave enough to go after the sheep and make them do what the farmer wants.

Sheep are much bigger than dogs so it takes courage for a collie to order them about. The dogs mustn't frighten the sheep by barking at them or biting them. Everything must be done in a very calm way. There is a lot for a sheepdog to know about making sheep do what they are told and my parents were very skilled at it.

My brothers were big and strong and when we were puppies we were always racing and chasing about together. I was much smaller than them and was often left behind in our games. I couldn't run as fast or jump as high but I always joined in, and we had so much fun I can't tell you.

My brothers were called Badger, Joey and Stan. Their coats were a mixture of black and white. Badger had the typical bold white stripe down the front of his face that many Border collies have, and that badgers have too - which was how he got his name!

My coat is mostly black with a white front. You can just see the shadow of a white stripe on my nose. In those days I was called Pixie. They chose that name because I have a little pointed face and it reminded them of a pixie.

From an early age my brothers and I wanted to learn to herd sheep. Even when we were quite small pups we would try to copy what our parents did. We tried to practice on the chickens but when they saw us coming they ran away, so we had to take it in turns to round up each other. We would run round in big circles, then drop down on to our bellies and creep forward towards our target. It was a great game. We took it for granted that when we grew up we would all be expert sheepdogs.

At last the great day came when we were sent out with our parents to start learning to work with real sheep. My brothers took to it immediately and soon they became very good at it. It was never that easy for me. Being so much smaller than my brothers, the sheep seemed enormous to me and there were so many. I was always nervous of them. I never believed I could make a flock of such big animals do what I told them.

I tried hard to learn all the farmer's commands and I could remember a lot of them, but when it came to putting them into practice it didn't work. The sheep simply wouldn't obey me. The farmer knew I was doing my best. He liked me; in fact I was always a bit of a favourite with him, but it was obvious I was never going to be any good at herding sheep.

I was so sad that I had failed at what I had always wanted to do. It was lucky for me that the farmer had a soft spot in his heart for little Pixie because I've heard that some farmers simply shoot a dog like me. Why keep an animal that can't work for its living?

When my parents retired from working and left the farm my three brothers took over from them. I was worried in case I would be sent away too but I was allowed to stay and we were always given enough food to go round between us all, me included.

We four dogs lived in the big, old barn where we had been born. It was snug and warm among the bales of straw. Often we would come in on wet days, covered in mud from the fields or the yard, and roll in the straw to dry our coats. Our food was thrown down on the ground for us and we drank from a bucket of water. It was a good life.

At night we would snuggle down together and sleep in a warm nest we had made for ourselves. Because of all the straw lying about, the barn doors never closed properly. Sometimes we would hear noises in the dark from the direction of the hen house. We would all rush out to scare away whatever creature was upsetting our chickens – usually a fox.

During the day I missed my brothers when they were out in the fields working the sheep but I did my best to make myself useful.

There were feral cats on the farm, rough and semi-wild, that lived in corners of the barn and hunted rats and mice. The farmer's wife had a pet cat named Hector. He was very big with fluffy, white and brown fur. Hector had a cat flap in the back door for his own personal use. I kept a sharp lookout for any of the feral cats. If I saw one I stalked it, using all my sheepdog skills, and made sure it was seen off pretty fast before it got near that cat flap.

Whenever any chickens strayed down by the front gate looking for something to peck at, I would practice my rounding up and kindly but firmly escort them back to their patch of dirt behind the barn.

There were always wellington boots left lying about outside the farmhouse door. I would go round and count them and make a note of where they were. People were always saying they were missing a boot, so I was able to help them look for it.

Not many strangers came our way. I would patrol the farmyard and if anyone did arrive at the gate I would bark as loudly as I could so the farmer's wife knew someone was there. Our few regular visitors were always welcome – they often had a biscuit in their pocket for me.

The farm workers were all kind to me. At lunchtime they would come into the barn and sit on a bale of straw to eat their sandwiches and they very often shared them with me. I would get a crust of bread or a bit of apple core. My favourite of all was crisps!

Life went on in the same sweet, simple way for years and years. The seasons came and went. Apart from the demands of the time of year everything remained much the same. There would be more lettuce in the sandwich fillings in the summer and sometimes in winter the men brought soup in a flask. Otherwise, the daily routine never varied.

Then came a time when a lot more visitors started coming to the farm. They would go into the house for a while and then walk out and have a good look around the outbuildings and talk to the farmer for a long time, asking all kinds of questions. This happened again and again with different groups of people until it became clear that something was going on.

At the time I was only mildly curious. People did things for their own good reasons that dogs didn't need to bother about. Whatever was happening with all these visitors, it wasn't anything to do with me.

How wrong could I be?

Chapter 3 – All Change

The truth was that the farm was up for sale. The farmer was retiring and moving away to a bungalow that had a small garden. We were sad that he was going because he was a good man.

He obviously couldn't take his livestock with him, so the sheep were staying as part of the sale. It seemed to us that if the new owner was having the flock he would want to have the sheepdogs too, so my brothers were pretty confident they would be staying on.

Nobody knew what was going to happen to me. It wasn't as if I was the farmer's pet dog. If I had been, he would have taken me with him. But there were no plans for me to go to the bungalow so it seemed I had been included in the sale to the new owner, even though I wasn't likely to be of much use to him.

Naturally, we expected changes when the new man came, although we had no idea what they would be. The farm seemed to be working pretty well as it was, so far as we could see, but people do like to put their own personal stamp on things. We waited to see what would happen.

It didn't take long to find out that the new man was a very different personality from the old farmer, who had been kind and easy-going. He was impatient and grouchy, not a man who was good at getting the best out of other people. Nothing ever worked right for him or was done quickly enough. He gave the farm workers a hard time of it, always grumbling at them. They took to gulping their sandwiches as fast as they could because he said they spent too long sitting down in the barn. They used to be full of jokes and good humour but they become grim-faced and silent whenever their new employer was around.

He was equally grumpy with the dogs, never giving a word of praise or a pat on the head, which means so much. He couldn't fault my brothers for the job they did with the sheep, but he soon came to believe I was a waste of space. He felt he had been cheated because he had paid for four useful dogs and only got three.

I was no longer allowed to roam about the yard. Visitors could go ungreeted, the cat flap be left unguarded and chickens could stray, so far as he was concerned. He cleared away the piles of straw around the barn doors and shut them tight with me on the inside. That was the end of my liberty.

The new man's evil temper seemed to have several causes. He had paid more money than he could really afford to buy the farm and now he was in debt. He couldn't afford to pay his bills and he couldn't pay his workers' wages. His wife got very angry about the mess he had got into and walked out on him. Within a few months of buying the farm, he had no choice but to sell it again.

This time, everything went, including the sheep. When the lorry came to fetch them I managed to force aside a loose plank of wood and squirm out of the barn. I stood barking by the gate as the lorry drove away with the flock of sheep plus Badger, Joey and Stan on board. I knew I would never see my three brothers again.

My barking got me into trouble. I was quickly returned to the barn and the door slammed shut. Without my brothers for company the barn became a prison. I couldn't bear to be locked in, on my own. I searched for every crack where I could to get out. My owner was furious. He went round hammering back all the loose boards, but for every one he replaced, I found another that I could pull back with my teeth or scrabble at with my paws. I had a knack for getting out through the smallest hole.

It was midsummer now and stifling hot in the barn. I kept escaping but I only made matters worse for myself. My owner came into the yard and grabbed me. He dragged me back into the barn, put a chain round my neck and nailed the other end to the barn wall. Then he went out and slammed the door shut.

I had never had anything round my neck in my life and the chain drove me nearly mad. I was a dog that was used to running free around the yard or over the fields. To be chained up was terrifying. I was in a state of panic. I couldn't stop panting. I clawed at the chain, tried to chew at it, but all I did was hurt my mouth. I had no way to get it off my neck and no way to move from the wall where the chain was fastened.

All my life I had gone out into the yard to pee or poo. Now, when it became necessary to do either of those things, I couldn't get outside. I tried hard to hold it, but it was just impossible. I had to do it right there, where I was tied up. Then, because the chain wasn't long enough for me to move away from the mess I had made, I had to sit in it. When I was finally so tired that I needed to sleep, I had to lay down in it, worn out, lonely, humiliated and dirty.

The barn that had been my birthplace and my happy home had now become my prison. Days passed. I was convinced that I had been left there to die. Nobody came to give me any food. There was a little water left in the bucket, which I could just reach, but I had soon finished the last of it. I stretched as far as the chain would allow me, snuffling about for a scrap of anything to eat.

I did discover something small and hard which I thought might be a crust of dry bread. I crunched down on it, but it was a stone and I broke my tooth. All I managed to find was the carcass of a dead mouse. It was disgusting, but I was so hungry that I ate it. I was desperate for a drink of water. That week was the worst of my life.

Chapter 4 – Rescue

I had given up all hope of leaving the barn alive when suddenly the door opened and my owner came in. Without a word he put a loop of rope round my neck instead of the chain and pulled me out of the barn behind him. I was weak and confused so I didn't resist. I simply followed him outside into the sunshine. He took me over to the other side of the yard where there was a tap in the wall. He turned on the water and pointed the hose at me.

The taste of the water in my mouth was the most marvellous thing, and it felt wonderful to have all the filth and stink washed off me. I shook myself to dry my coat and the man shouted at me because I had splashed water all over him. I was glad!

Next, he took me and put me in his car. I had never been in a car before and I was very frightened. He put me on the floor behind his seat and tied the rope to the door. It was horrible being bumped about and swung round corners. The drive seemed to go on forever but at last we stopped and he got me out of the car.

I could hear a lot of dogs barking but I couldn't see them. We went into a big room with a floor that wasn't earth or straw. It was flat and slippery and I was afraid I would fall over.

A lady with a badge came and spoke to the man. He said I was a stray dog and would they take me? When she agreed he put the rope in her hand, turned on his heel and left. I was glad to see the last of him. He was a horrible man and also a liar. I wasn't a stray. Why did he say that?

Everything about this place he had brought me to made me anxious. What kind of place was it? I couldn't smell any farmyard scents. Why were all those dogs barking? What would the badge lady do to me? I didn't know what to expect.

The badge-lady seemed to know I was frightened of her and she didn't try to touch me. She spoke to me in a kinder tone than my owner had. She put a little food in a bowl and offered it to me. I woofed it down in a couple of mouthfuls. I was so hungry I could have eaten the dish as well! There was a big bowl of water by the door so I was able to have a drink too.

The badge-lady opened a red door and immediately I knew where all the noise was coming from. On the other side of the door were rows of pens, all full of dogs and most of them were barking, whining or howling. Their voices sounded frantic. These were not happy dogs.

The badge-lady tried to lead me by the rope towards a pen but I didn't want to go. This seemed as bad a prison as the one I had just left — worse, even, because of all the distressing cries. There would be no peace here for me, alongside all these troubled dogs.

The badge-lady called a helper who came and put a bowl of food in the pen and I had no choice then but to go in, if I wanted to eat. I think she knew how upset I was because when she slipped the rope off she stroked my head before she shut the door on me and left.

I looked round the pen. The back wall was wooden. There were heavy iron bars on the other three sides with a corrugated iron roof. The floor was made of hard stuff, very rough and cold. My pen was between two others. There was a dog in each. I was very glad they were not making a noise. They were both curled up in a tight ball with their nose under their tail as if trying to shut out everything that was going on around them. I decided to do the same.

I had been fed here and it seemed I was expected to sleep here so I had to face the fact that this was now my home. I didn't like it, but I was not sorry to be back among other dogs even though the atmosphere was very stressful. I missed my brothers and miserable dogs were better than no company.

From time to time the badge-lady or one of her helpers came with a collar and lead and took one of the dogs away. Sometimes they came back, sometimes they didn't. That made me fearful. What happened to those dogs? Was I on some kind of death row, waiting to be called to my execution. When would it be my turn to make that fateful journey?

It felt like forever but it was probably less than a week before one of the helpers came to my pen. I didn't want him to put the collar round my neck so I hung back in a corner, but it was no good. The dreaded collar went on and he gently pulled me behind him towards the red door.

When we went through we were back in the room with the slippery floor. There was nobody there except a lady I had never seen before, sitting in a chair.

The helper who had hold of my lead told her I was very shy so I probably wouldn't come to her. She looked at me and smiled. She didn't get up or walk towards me or call me. She just sat there smiling and holding out her hands. There was something about her that I felt able to trust. I was sure she wasn't going to let anyone kill me. Not just yet.

I started to walk towards her. The helper dropped my lead and it trailed on the ground behind me. I walked right up to her and put my head on her knee. She smiled at me so sweetly then, I felt sure everything would be all right.

The helper laughed and said I had made a liar of him – he had not expected me to be so brave.

I stayed beside the lady, leaning against her legs. She stroked me and tickled behind my ears. She talked to me in a soft voice and told me I was beautiful and I licked her hand. It was so wonderful to have been let out of my prison and brought into this quiet room to spend a little time with this nice lady.

I thought to myself, I don't care if they take me from here to my death. I shall think about this and how beautiful it was to be made such a fuss of.

And if I'm lucky enough to escape that for now, and they take me back to my pen, remembering this lovely time will keep my spirits up when I'm curled in a ball trying to shut out the world.

To my surprise the nice lady asked me if I wanted to go for a little walk outside with her. I was very willing to go. She held my lead loosely and I walked beside her, looking up at her face all the time. She talked gently to me and didn't try to make me hurry. I was very happy to follow her back to the building.

The helper who had brought me out was waiting in the doorway. The lady told him she was impressed by how well behaved I had been on my lead. When I heard that, I felt pretty impressed with myself. I had always hated being on a lead and struggled to get away.

The nice lady's car was parked just by the door. She pointed to it and asked me if I would like to go home with her. I couldn't believe it! She was willing to take me away from this prison camp? Of course I wanted to go! I could not have wagged my tail any harder.

She laughed and bent down and patted me. She understood I was telling her 'yes'.

Then I understood where the other dogs had gone. They had not been killed. People had taken them away to live with them. This place was not so bad after all. It was stressful here but the badge-lady and her helpers made sure none of the dogs had to stay for long. As soon as they could, they found a person to take each dog away and give them a new home.

We went back into the room and I sat by my favourite lady's legs while she filled in some forms. The badge-lady explained that I had been brought in as a stray without a name so they had called me Meg. I don't know why they chose that. The forms were soon completed and we went outside again. The lady opened the hatch at the back of her car and one of the helpers lifted me into a cage that was waiting for me there.

Before we set off, the nice lady came and spoke to me. She told me I was her dog now. She was going to drive me to her house. There would be just the two of us and we had all the time in the world to get to know each other.

It was only the second time I had ever been in a car.

The cage I was in had much thinner bars than the pen. It was big enough for me to lie down but small enough to keep me from sliding about when the car went round corners. I felt safe in it. Still, the journey was rather frightening. As we pulled on to the main road I looked out of the back window and immediately wished I hadn't.

Very few cars came up the lane to the farm. It was narrow and rutted and so those that came drove very slowly. The cars I could see now were going so fast, flashing by in all directions. And there were so many – I had never imagined there were so many cars in the world. I was sure one of them was going to smash into us.

I was so anxious I peed in the bottom of my cage. Then I felt terrible. This kind lady had rescued me and I had repaid her by making a mess in her car. What would she say? Perhaps she would turn round and drive me straight back again.

When we arrived at her house I was shaking with nervousness. My lady lifted the hatch and opened my cage. She noticed that I had peed but she didn't make any fuss. She told me she would soon clean it up. She said she realised I must have been very frightened to do that. She didn't want me to be frightened. We were home now, where she would look after me.

I looked round to see what my new home would be. My heart sank. We were on a street with houses all along both sides. There was not a tree or an open space of green anywhere. The ground under my feet was not earth or grass, just hard, cold stone. There were cars parked all along the road. How was I ever going to think of this array of brick and metal as home?

My lady took my lead. She helped me to jump down from the back of the car and gently led me to the door of the house where I was going to live.

Chapter 5 – New Home

We went through a door into a corridor lined with bricks. It seemed to be a passageway between two of the houses. At the end we went through a gate into a small yard with a floor of hard stone. There were some wheelie bins and big flowerpots with plants in them. I looked around and didn't see anything I liked. Most of all, I wanted to have a good sniff about.

My owner seemed to understand what I wanted. She dropped my lead and let me move around and smell things. Just beyond the bins there was a little gate fixed with a hook. A path led on up the garden to an arch, with flowers growing on the other side of it. It was a narrow garden but went back quite a long way to a brick wall at the end.

Bricks everywhere. I didn't like the scent of them. I tried to find something that smelled of earth or straw or animals but there was nothing. There wasn't a barn, or even a pen. Where was I going to sleep?

Across the yard there was a glass door leading into the house. My owner opened it and indicated that I was to go inside.

I had never been in a house before. It took a lot of persuading for me to enter. I was very suspicious. I disliked it even more than outside in the little yard. The floor was shiny, like the one I had just left behind. It was slippery and difficult to walk on.

This was a narrow room with wooden cupboards right down to the floor. It was the kitchen. My kind lady filled a bowl with water and put it down on the floor for me. I lapped up a little, because I was very dry, but I didn't feel relaxed enough to drink properly.

A door led from the kitchen into a much bigger room. There were a lot of things in there I didn't recognise. Worst of all, when I walked forward the floor turned into something soft that my feet almost sank into. It was horrible! With earth or straw under my feet, I could sense things about the place where I was but this stuff gave me no clues. It felt completely dead, stretching right to the far wall; in fact the whole floor was covered with it. There was no sound even when my owner walked on it.

I went a few steps into the room, because I didn't want to seem ungrateful, but I didn't go any further. I really appreciated my lovely owner not trying to make me do what I didn't want to. She left me to look and sniff around, get used to the place and decide where I wanted to sit down.

There were a lot of objects in the room which reminded me a bit of the bales of hay in the barn. My owner sat down on one of them like the farm workers used to. She put her things down on another one. There was a big box that had voices coming out of it and flickering lights all over the front. My owner sat looking at it. I thought it was scary and kept well away from it. I chose a small space in a corner to lie down and curl up.

The main thing I noticed about the room was how incredibly noisy it was. I could hear all kinds of strange sounds which seemed to stop and start at random. I have extremely sensitive hearing and I was accustomed to living in a very quiet place. In the barn I could hear the spiders spinning their webs.

Here, I was surrounded by things going pop and boing and brrrrrrr and ding-dong and ping. They were all unnatural, mechanical noises.

Long afterwards, when I had got used to the hot water boiler switching on and off, the kettle boiling and the microwave beeping, the telephone, the chiming clock, E-mails arriving and the door bell, I thought how silly I had been to be afraid, but I was experiencing all these things for the first time in my life and I didn't know if something was going to hurt me.

During the rest of that day I watched my owner come and go between one room and the other. She had brought home a big bag of dried dog food in the car and at teatime she called me through to the kitchen and offered me a bowl of it.

I went because I was hungry but as soon as I had eaten and had a drink of water, I went back to my safe corner. As long as I could see where my owner was, I didn't want to move from there.

Later on in the evening she called me and took me outside on to the little yard. I followed, wondering if she thought I would do a pee or a poo, but I was far too unsettled by these strange surroundings to do either.

When it got dark she said it was bedtime. I supposed I would sleep where I had been curled up since I arrived. But no, she opened a door in the corner of the room and called me to follow her.

I was completely baffled. The floor behind the door wasn't a proper floor. It seemed to be a lot of blocks all piled on top of each other. There was no way it would be safe to walk on those. You would have to climb onto them. Besides, they were covered with the same soft stuff that I didn't like, which I found out later was called carpet. I looked but I wouldn't go through the door. I ran back to my corner.

Somehow my owner managed to climb up on these blocks, which she called stairs, and down again, without hurting herself. When she came back she had changed her clothes and was carrying a blanket. She put it down on a thing that looked like several bales of hay pushed together.

She put out all the lights except one. Then she spread the blanket out and lay down and pulled the blanket over herself. She called me to her. I went and laid down beside her. Her head was not very far from mine. I reached forward and licked her face. She smiled and stroked my head and told me it was time to go to sleep.

Then she put out the last of the lights, wished me goodnight and closed her eyes.

I did the same. In the darkness the mechanical sounds seemed louder than ever – futt! futt! whirrrr! ping! The worst was one that happened every half an hour. There was a kind of winding up sound and then something like a hammer hitting a gong. Sometimes it was just once, sometimes it was repeated over and over. Just as I began to get into a doze, off it went again. I gave up any hope of going to sleep.

I lay there warm, dry, fed and watered, and I had a long think. On the plus side, here I was with a kind person who had promised to look after me and been as good as her word. She spoke gently to me, stroked and patted me, had even gone to sleep beside me. If the price of such affection was to get used to life under her roof, then it was not such a big price to pay.

I vowed I would try to meet whatever new challenges came my way with as much courage as I could and not repay her by showing fear and anxiety all the time.

Things did not get off to a good start next morning. I should have taken the opportunity she offered me for a pee the previous night.

By the time she was ready to get up I was absolutely bursting and when a new, very loud noise made me jump, I did a pee right there in the room.

It was a small box that startled me. It was making a ringing sound, over and over again, really loud. I backed away because I thought it was going to explode but my owner ignored it. She opened the back door and took me out on to the yard and left me for a few minutes. I was very glad to be able to relieve myself outside.

When she fetched me in the ringing noise had stopped. She had cleaned up behind me so there was no trace of my accident to be seen. She wasn't cross with me and in fact she gave me a cuddle and told me she loved me.

I thought only mothers loved you. I decided from now on to think of her as my second mum.

Chapter 6 – Walkies

Keeping my resolve not to show fear wasn't as easy as I had hoped. On my first full day with my new mum she decided to take me out for a walk. I was petrified. For one thing, I was on a lead again and that always caused me stress.

First, we went outside the house and on to the street. There were about two dozen houses on either side, all attached to each other, all looking exactly alike. If I got lost, how would I ever find my way back to the right house?

I didn't want to go anywhere. I squirmed and tossed my head and tried to get my collar off. I tried to lie down. I pulled and tugged and did everything I could think of to avoid having to walk along that street. We got past about two houses and my mum brought me back and we went indoors again.

To my amazement she praised me and told me what a brave dog I was. She seemed to know how hard it was for me to do what she was asking. When she took me out again later in the day, we went past the same two houses and then the next one as well.

We practically held a celebration a few days later, when we got to the corner of the street.

It had been hard and I had been trembling with fear, but it felt like such an achievement. Nothing bad had happened, I had got there and got back again. I kept telling myself if I could walk to the end of our street, I could walk to the end of the next street. And the next, and the next, until I could walk anywhere.

Just about that time I started to feel ill. It turned out I had caught kennel cough when I was in the rescue centre but it had taken a while for it to come out. It was like a person having a very bad cold. My throat was sore, I started sneezing and coughing and my nose was blocked up.

Dogs have big noses so when they get full of mucus, it's a bit nasty. My mum kept a close watch on me and every time she thought I was going to shake my head to clear my nose, I got a handful of tissues clamped over my face. She encouraged me to blow, but dogs can't blow their nose. I was very uncomfortable for about a week and then it cleared up completely.

Despite my kennel cough, we kept going out for our walks and mum set us a fresh goal every couple of days. First, it was across the car park, then past the cricket club, then past the school and finally in at the entrance to the old railway path.

We had one bad setback, the day we met a double-decker bus and the bin lorry. The bus was waiting outside the school with the engine throbbing and lights blinking on its sides. The bin lorry was on the opposite side of the road. No other vehicle could have got past between them. Yellow lights were flashing and wheelie bins were flying up in the air as they were emptied automatically into the back of the lorry, clanking and banging. I cowered against the school railings, too terrified to walk past. Mum quickly turned back and took me home.

The old railway path is about three miles long. It's off the road so there are no cars there at all. Where we join it, there is a wide grass border on each side with bushes and trees. It's the closest thing to countryside near my new home.

For me to walk on the lead as far as the entrance to the railway path took two weeks of determined effort. It's five minutes from our house.

I was feeling better about being on a lead but wearing a collar still bothered me. I had such bad memories of being tied up by my neck.

Right from the start my mum insisted I had to wear a soft collar with an identity disc on it. All dogs are supposed to, even if they're microchipped, like I was at the rescue centre. On the farm no one ever bothered about identity discs. I don't suppose they even knew it was a rule.

My mum knew how distressed I was when she put a lead on my collar so she got me a special 'halter' to fit over my face, so that my lead could be attached to that instead. I always wore that when I went out and I preferred it.

The only way on to the railway path is via a very thin gap in the railings that is just big enough for a person to pass. It's about possible to get a push-bike through but it would stop anyone with a motorbike getting on to the path.

This gap has always been a trial for me, even though there's no gate on it. I'm not good with narrow entrances. I can't help it.

I'm the same with any door or gate. I'm always expecting it to slam shut on me. I have to dive through as quickly as I can. It's a bad habit, especially if you're on a lead, because you pull the person holding you. I try not to do it but often I still do. My mum is very patient with me.

Having a big expanse of grass where I could go every day made a lot of difference to me. I had been very unhappy about relieving myself on the yard but now I didn't mind if I could do it on the grass. My mum always has poo bags in her pocket and there are red disposal bins all along the route of the railway path.

I still had problems with my early morning and late night pee. My mum knew how I hated doing it on the yard. Twice a day she took me up to the far end of the garden and tried to persuade me to do it there but I still couldn't. There were not enough familiar smells to make me feel comfortable about it.

So early every morning and last thing every evening my mum put on her outdoor clothes and off we went to the railway path so I could pee on the grass. When we got there I had to sniff around for a while before I felt relaxed enough to do it. Every time, it was a round trip of a quarter of an hour, sometimes in pouring rain, but my mum stuck with it.

On those wet days, when she first got up, she'd pull on her wellies and put her waterproofs on over her pyjamas to take me to the top of the garden, and still she'd end up having to get dressed and take me to the railway path before I would pee, but she never got cross.

It was the same just before bed. Even if her eyes were drooping in front the TV, she would get all her dog-walking gear on and take me out, first up the garden but eventually up the road for that final comfort stop.

As the weather changed and it became frosty and bitterly cold, I gave myself a good talking to.

I really did know my way around the top garden now and there was no reason at all why I couldn't do what she wanted. She had even tried to teach me to pee when she told me to, by giving me a treat every time I did it. I decided the time had come to repay all her patience and stop demanding to be taken up the road.

So, one early morning when she took me into the garden in her dressing gown and overcoat and told me to pee, I did it. She was so pleased, I got lots of praise and hugs. I felt proud that I'd taken the first step towards independence. I've done my pee ever since in that part of the garden, whenever she tells me.

One day I'm going to start running up to the top garden on my own so my mum doesn't have to come out of the house to supervise me, but right now I still don't feel able to do it unless she comes up the garden with me.

I'm sure other dogs can pee without thinking about it but it has been a big thing for me and has taken me months to overcome.

I feel so vulnerable in this new world that I don't understand. For me, coming to live here has been like being transported to an alien planet. I need to learn, step by step, what everybody around me seems to know by instinct. I am unsure all the time, feeling my way, having to check often whether I'm doing right or wrong because here, all the rules are different from where I came from.

Dogs are not like people. Basically, we're pack animals. When we're born we automatically know whether we're a leader or a follower. We settle into our role and that's it. We never change our position in the pecking order of the pack. I've always been a follower. My brother, Badger, was leader of our pack of four and I followed him for seven years. In this new life my mum is the leader of our pack of two – and she isn't a dog.

Dogs know by nature what we should do when we're all dogs together. When we're with people it's harder. We attach ourselves in the same way to our leader but we have to learn what's required of us by constantly watching and listening. I can tell so many things by my mum's tone of voice, the way she moves about, when her steps quicken, when she goes to a certain cupboard.

Having a routine to life makes it easier and my mum helps me by talking to me and telling me what's going on. She knows I can't grasp all the words she says but she knows I can understand things by the way she speaks, and she constantly reassures me.

One big problem for me is, if I can't see my mum, I don't know what I'm supposed to do next. That puts me in the terrible position of having to be the leader of a pack of one. I can't cope with that. It completely freaks me out. I panic. I just want to run away. I can't handle the responsibility.

She and I have two basic ways of dealing with being apart, depending on how long my mum is going to be gone. If she is going to leave the house for a long period of time, she puts me in my cage in the car and takes me with her. I know when she gets out of the car that she is certain to come back, so I'm perfectly happy to settle down and go to sleep until then.

If she's going to the local shops and will only be a little while, then she leaves me on the yard. When she gets out her shopping trolley, I know she is only going to be gone half an hour or so. I don't much like being left, but I can manage it if I'm outdoors. I try very hard not to cry or bark or howl and usually my mum comes back before I start feeling over-anxious.

My mum hardly ever leaves me indoors because I really don't react well to being left alone in the house. She wouldn't let me roam about loose because it would be dangerous for me, so it means being put in my big cage with the door shut.

I don't mind being in my cage so long as mum is there, but as soon as she leaves I start having a panic attack. If there is anything soft in the cage, I can relieve my feelings a bit by ripping it up. It helps to get my teeth into something and tear at it. If there's nothing soft, I will gnaw at the bars, even if means hurting my mouth.

I know it's going to mean a lot of work for my mum and me to overcome my separation anxiety. She knows I can't help it and I'm not being a bad dog.

My mum says there is no such thing as a bad dog, only owners who don't know enough or care enough to look after their dog properly.

My mum isn't a bad owner. She deals with me and my difficulties as well as she can, and will do everything possible to make me more confident, but I'm afraid it will take a long time before she and I manage to work out a solution to this particular problem together.

Chapter 7 – Friends

Another thing that took me two weeks to conquer when I first arrived was the stairs. I watched my mum go up and down them several times a day. She knew I liked to see where she was, so she hoped that if she went upstairs I would be persuaded to follow her, but however hard she tried to entice me up, I wouldn't go.

Eventually it happened when one of her friends was in the house. With my mum in front of me and her friend behind me, I very gingerly tried putting my paws on the first step, and to my amazement I made it to the top. It was interesting to see more rooms up there. Going down was difficult but I did it on my own. Mum made a great fuss of me and praised me so I felt I had done something really special.

Later that night, thinking about it, I realised my mum had her bedroom upstairs. She had been bringing her blanket downstairs and sleeping on the sofa every night so that I wasn't alone, because I was too scared to follow her upstairs. I felt ashamed then, and made up my mind to practice climbing the stairs until I could do it confidently.

I don't know what they had told her about me at the rescue centre, but my mum didn't seem surprised that I was taking a long time to settle in, and she was prepared to help me in every way she could. She clearly loves Border collies and was willing to do everything in her power to make this one happy.

One of the things she did that pleased me was change my name. She didn't think Meg suited me any more than I did. She decided to call me Cassie. It was quite close to Pixie, and I liked it. I very soon learned to come when she called me. In fact, I did it from the very first time.

Another nice thing my mum did was introduce me to friends. There are three dogs living just across the road.

Buster is a black Labrador and next door to him is Coco, a chocolate Lab. My best friend is a sturdy, good-natured terrier called Eddie who lives right opposite us. The fur on his face is blond and curly, changing to straighter and darker over his back. He carries his tail high, like a question mark. Eddie was a rescue dog too and his family all love him to pieces. Eddie's house was the first one I went into after ours. Now we visit each other often. It was very strange the first time I went into Eddie's house because it's completely different from our house. I am always made extremely welcome so I like to go Eddie-visiting.

Early every morning Eddie's mum takes us both out for a short walk, and then again in the evening. My mum takes us for a longer walk in the middle of the day. Eddie is very well behaved on the lead and comes when he is called when he's off the lead.

My mum calls Eddie 'Mr Sniff' because that's what he really enjoys doing on our walks. All dogs use their nose a lot and Eddie is especially keen on smells. Dogs' whole lives are dominated by scent. If you imagine a person's sense of smell as the size of a postage stamp, then by comparison a dog's sense of smell is the size of a table cloth. We learn so much from using our nose.

On the old railway path I can tell every creature that has passed by in the previous twenty-four hours. A lot of dogs are exercised there, and they all leave their mark by doing a pee in their favourite place. People ride bikes and horses along the path. It's used by cats and rats and moles and voles and they all leave their own distinctive smell. It's one of the things that makes it an endlessly interesting place to walk because there's something different to smell every time we go.

I've made a lot of friends among the regulars. Very few of the dogs we meet are unfriendly. Most of them just want to wag their tails and have a sniff at each other.

To begin with, my mum used to put me on an extending lead when we left the traffic behind and began our off-road walk. Neither of us had ever had any experience of using one before and I have to say we weren't very good at it. We got tangled up round bushes and gateposts and each other a fair few times, and once or twice I nearly tripped my mum over.

One day, about a month later, we went in the car to meet my mum's friend and her Border collie, Merlin. He's a big, handsome dog and very obedient.

We went for a walk together at a small park well away from the road and mum's friend suggested letting me off the lead. She was sure I wouldn't run away and Merlin was there to keep an eye on me.

Mum agreed and took the lead off. It was so wonderful to be free, I can't tell you. I made sure I didn't let mum out of my sight and I came back as soon as she called me, every time.

That was a great walk because now Merlin and I are friends, and I run free off the lead every time mum takes me out. I was so proud the next time we went back to the railway path and I didn't have a lead on. My mum threw the extending lead in the bin.

I still had to have a lead for walking on the street. I've got a long lead in a lovely bright red, with stripes that show up in cars' headlights. After a few weeks, Mum replaced my 'halter' with a red double-check-chain collar that she slips on and off over my head. She always carries a shoulder bag on our walks so she has somewhere to put my collar and lead when she takes them off, along with the poo bags and some treats.

My bright red lead was a present from Digby's mum. He's another of my friends. He's a very small, coal-black Patterdale terrier. He loves to jump up on his mum's lap for a cuddle. He's very lightweight so he's good at jumping. I don't see him often because he lives a long way away. Digby was also a rescue dog.

One of Digby's favourite pastimes is chasing rabbits. Once, he followed one right down into its burrow, but the hole narrowed suddenly and he got stuck. After trying every other way to get him free, he finally had to be pulled out by his tail.

Another ex-rescue friend of mine is Daisy. She's a dainty brown and black terrier who looks as if she could run like a whippet. Occasionally, my mum goes to places where I can't go and I can't be left to wait in the car because it would be too long to leave me. Then I go to Daisy's house and her dad looks after me.

Daisy loves toys. I just don't understand toys at all. Kind people have given me toys but I don't know what I'm supposed to do with them. The ones that squeak frighten me to death!

My mum knows this so she makes up games for me to play without toys.

Some days she divides up my dinner between my dinner bowl and half a dozen little picnic dishes and hides them all around the house. I have to run about and find them all if I want my dinner. I love that game. She thinks of lots of different places to hide them so the game is never the same twice.

In the garden in the summer, when the lawn was due for a mow, mum would scatter a handful of treats into the long grass for me to run about and search for.

We have another game when we go on our walks. Sometimes we branch off the old railway path and walk on an open track between fields. The track goes on for miles so my mum has made the limit of our walk an oak tree that stands beside the track. When she reaches out and touches the tree, that's the signal for me to turn round and dash back up the track as fast as I can. She makes me wait and doesn't always touch the same branch, so I have to watch her like a hawk.

I like my games better than toys. Daisy chases balls and plays tug with a rope and gnaws at plastic bones. She has a whole box of toys and gets them out one by one to show me when I go to her house.

Daisy's dad is very kind and makes a big fuss of me and gives me little treats.

When I first came to live with my mum there was a gate from the yard to the path leading up the garden. It was a very light gate and it simply fixed over a hook on the gatepost. I watched my mum open it once or twice and it seemed ever so easy, so when she left me on the yard one day I opened it myself and went for a wander up the garden.

The garden wall is quite low and there were some people in the garden next door so I jumped over and went to say hello to them. They were very nice and looked after me until my mum came home.

My mum explained to me that the gate was there to stop me going up the garden and visiting the neighbours.

At the weekend, Daisy's dad came with his tool box to put up a new gate. It was bigger than the old one and had a latch that I couldn't open. The yard filled up with wood shavings and mum made cups of tea, and eventually the gate was finished and in place. The trouble was, I was on one side of it and my mum was on the other, so I squashed myself flat to the ground and squirmed underneath it to be with her.

My mum and Daisy's dad laughed so much they spilled their tea. They hadn't expected I would be able to get under the gate. They said I reminded them of a limbo dancer. I'd just done what I used to do when the farmer locked me in the barn and I wanted to get out.

I'm not fat and I'm quite supple so I've never had trouble squeezing through small gaps.

Daisy's dad came back the next day with another piece of wood and nailed it on to the bottom of the gate so it nearly reaches the ground. You'd have to be an earthworm to get under there now.

Chapter 8 – Training

I have four other friends named Esther, Ruby, Lily and Zak. We all joined the obedience training class together and we go once a week to the local church hall to practice our exercises. We're working towards the bronze award of the Kennel Club's Good Citizen Dog Scheme.

Wallace and Gromit promote the Good Citizen Scheme but I don't think any of us will ever get to be as smart as Gromit!

My friend Esther is a Spanish water dog and the thing everybody loves about her is her coat. She is one mass of black curls. You have to push her hair back off her face to see her eyes. She's about the same size as me but is much younger, only about six months old. She's very friendly and we're always pleased to see each other. We sometimes meet on our walks, too.

Ruby is a Rottweiler and is also young. She's very friendly and lively. She isn't very tall but she's heavily built with a big head. She has lovely golden markings on her sleek, dark fur.

The thing with Ruby is, she doesn't know she's a big dog. She wags her tail and throws herself at people and other dogs, and wants to lick them to death. She seems quite amazed when she practically knocks them over.

Rottweilers are very strong dogs so they have to be taught how to behave. Ruby picked up all her exercises very quickly and enjoys doing them.

Ruby gives the lie to the idea that Rottweilers are aggressive. She is as soft as a brush and as well behaved and affectionate as any other dog that is loved and well looked after. A dog of any breed can be turned into a fierce, snarling monster if that's the way it's treated by its owner.

Lily's a German shepherd. She was a baby when she started classes but she has grown before our eyes over the weeks of our course. She's a lovely dog with a beautifully marked coat. Lily is a quick learner and loves the training.

Zak keeps himself to himself. He's an enormous dog and he needs his own space but he does all his exercises just like we do.

He's an Akita which is a Japanese breed. His coat is almost entirely white. He carries his tail curled up over his back in two big loops and only uncurls it to wag it. As soon as he stops wagging, it snaps back again.

We have a huge range of dog breeds in our obedience class, working at different levels – some for their silver award and some for gold. Cherry is the smallest. She's a tiny Border terrier, light brown flecked with grey. The largest is Gandalf, a massive chestnut and white St Bernard.

We are all treated exactly the same and all have to practice our exercises until we can do them well. We watch and listen and work at them week by week until we can sit, wait, stay, go down, come when called and leave food untouched. We learn to walk on the lead without pulling, sit when our handler stops, allow our ears, eyes, mouth and paws to be examined, fetch a toy and give it up when asked.

Sometimes we work in pairs, sometimes we all stand round the room together in a big circle. Other times we line up either side of a central line, each dog facing alternately either left or right. We do this when we practice walking correctly through a door. We have to wait while our handler opens the door, tells us to come through, wait again while they close the door and then turn and repeat the exercise, remembering all those steps.

The hardest exercise is when we are sent away by our handler. That's much harder than coming to them when called. We have to leave them when they tell us and go to the other end of the room and lie down on our 'bed', which can be a cushion or a blanket, whatever our owner has chosen. Mine is a square of fleece with gripper material on the back to stop it sliding on the shiny floor.

Going away isn't part of the bronze award. We won't have to do it until we get to the gold, but because it's such a hard exercise we've started learning it now, just moving a little way away from our handler, because it will take time to work up to going the full distance from them.

You would expect to need ear plugs if you walked into a room full of dogs because they would all be barking, but that's not so. It's very rare for a dog to bark during our lessons. They're all concentrating too hard on trying to remember their exercises. The owners make more noise than the dogs do!

I really look forward to Wednesdays and can't wait to go to training class. I love doing all the exercises. It wasn't like that to begin with, though. When I walked into that hall for the first time with my mum, I was terrified. There were so many people and so many dogs. As soon as my mum sat down I hid under her chair and sat quaking. It took me a few weeks to get my confidence to join in with the other dogs, but they and their owners are all so friendly that I soon began to feel better about going.

I have one particular problem – Cherry. She is tiny, not much bigger than a large cat. She isn't unfriendly towards me, but neither is she particularly interested in me. But I can't take me eyes off her. She draws me to her like a magnet. I don't know if she reminds me of those cats I used to stalk and chase away from the cat flap, but I just feel a huge urge inside me to fix my eyes on her. It's what collies do – they stare at animals they are herding. It gives them focus for the task.

Unfortunately, staring can become excessive. It's said that with some collies you could set them to guard a paper bag, and twenty-four hours later they would still be in exactly the same place, never having taken their eyes off it.

I have this kind of trouble with Cherry. If she's in the room, I have to look at her. It's nothing to do with any interaction between us. She doesn't look back at me or even seem aware that I'm staring at her.

It's just me, giving her the Border collie 'eye', which is totally inappropriate and unwanted behaviour when we're trying to learn to be obedient. While I'm putting all my focus into watching Cherry, I can't concentrate on what I'm being taught.

Our trainer has helped my mum try to snap me out of this fixation on Cherry and sometimes I do manage to look away from her for a few minutes. Mum gives me a treat if I do. If, for some reason, Cherry isn't in the room I can give my full attention to learning whatever task we're being taught, and I feel much better about it.

When we go home, mum practises all the exercises with me and I can do them all, off pat. You would think I was a model student! But as soon as I get back into the room with Cherry and the other dogs, everything goes out of the window and I'm back to staring and forgetting my commands.

It isn't easy for my mum, because she likes to encourage and praise me, but she has to be really firm and tell me off when I go into 'stalk Cherry' mode. She changes her tone of voice then and I know she's cross with me, so I try harder to concentrate on her and what I'm supposed to be doing.

We both come back from our hour and a half of training feeling pretty exhausted. Mum makes herself a cup of tea. I'm usually fast asleep in my basket by the time the kettle has boiled.

Chapter 9 – Bad Dog

It was July when I first came to live with my mum. She could not have been kinder to me. She was always telling me what a good dog I was and praising me and encouraging me. She took me out for walks. She talked to me, sometimes she even sang to me. She's not a very good singer so I would really rather she didn't, but I think it's well meant. She cuddled me and stroked me, which I loved. She brushed me every day, which was a wonderfully relaxing experience.

After a few months I began to get over my nervousness and feel that I might be able to settle down to living in a house.

And then, one evening, the most dreadful thing happened. It was early November and the clocks had gone back so it got dark quite quickly. Mum had pulled the curtains earlier than usual and put the TV on with the sound turned up loud. We hadn't even had our tea when there was such a bang I nearly jumped out of my fur.

People outside in the adjoining gardens had started firing guns. At any rate, that's what it sounded like to me. I learned later that they're called fireworks. They explode with a deafening din and send shock waves through the air. I've told you that I have very sensitive hearing and it really hurt my ears.

I wanted it to stop. I ran about the sitting room, crying, trying to tell my mum she had to stop it, but she didn't. It went on and on, getting worse and worse. I couldn't stand the blasts and bangs. They sounded as if they were coming in the room. Mum kept talking to me but that wasn't any good. She had to make them stop. I kept telling her. But she didn't. She didn't even go outside and try.

I tried to get outside myself. I kept flinging myself at the glass door. Mum got hold of me and stopped me. She shut the door between the living room and the kitchen. Then she put my lead on and put one end of it under the leg of her chair. Well, I've told you what I'm like about being tied up. I was distressed enough already. It took me two bites to get through the lead. As soon as I was free I began rushing up and down the room, throwing myself at the wall at either end.

My mum got hold of me again and put me in my cage. I nearly went mad. I had to get free. I tore up every bit of bedding in the bottom of my cage. I just ripped and ripped at it, until it was in shreds. Then I started biting at the bars, crying, panting, dribbling and trembling, throwing myself about. My mum took me out of my cage and we finished up wrestling with each other, she trying to hold me and me trying to get away.

Why didn't my mum make them stop this terrible din? I thought my mum could do anything. I thought she loved me. All I could assume now was that I had been a very bad dog and this was my punishment. All the disobedient things I had done since I arrived, that my mum had told me were all right, must really have been terribly wicked and now I had to pay for them. I didn't think I was such a bad dog, but I must have been. Otherwise, why did I have to suffer like this?

I had never experienced anything so horrendous in my life before. Rather than go through any more of this, it would have been better if the farmer had shot me.

That terrible evening went on for hours. By bedtime I was completely exhausted. I think my mum was too. She was certainly upset. When we went upstairs she cuddled me and stroked me and tried to get me to go to sleep but I was still shaking. At last, I did fall asleep beside her bed, but every now and again there was another whoosh and I shot awake. We both had a sleepless few hours until at last it fell quiet outside and we both eventually went to sleep.

The next day, all was quiet. When I went into the garden I came across a lot of debris from the fireworks. It smelled bad and I passed it by, keeping as far away as I could. Mum repaired my lead, although it was much shorter now.

Things settled back to normal until a few weeks later when, to my horror, on New Year's Eve, there was another night of fireworks whizzing and banging. It wasn't quite so bad because they started much later and only lasted for about half an hour, around midnight.

A week or two before, my mum had bought a spray that she used all round my basket and cage. It smelled quite nice and made me feel good, but I still suffered because the explosions were so loud and so unexpected.

But it got me thinking, as I lay beside my mum's bed later that night. By spraying my basket she was trying to find a way to save me from being distressed and frightened.

She had bought that spray in advance so she must have known there would be another evening of noise that I would hate. I thought, perhaps this is something that happens every so often where I live now and my mum can't do anything about it. In that case, I wasn't being punished for being a bad dog.

I felt better about things then. I had been trying so hard to be a good dog. I thought I was beginning to understand what my mum wanted of me. I was learning how to please her by being obedient and respectful. She kept telling me I was doing well. I wanted that to be true, and not think I was impossibly bad and deserving of punishment.

Next morning, when it was time for me to give my mum the usual nudge and a lick to wake her up, I gave her a lot of extra licky kisses to let her know her good dog loves her very much.

Chapter 10 – Big Sisters

When I arrived in my new home there was this thing in the sitting room. I didn't know what it was so I gave it a wide berth. My mum told me it was my basket and encouraged me to try getting into it but I wouldn't, so she took it away. I was glad there was one fewer new thing for me to worry about.

After a couple of months the basket appeared back in the sitting room with a fleece blanket in it. Mum invited me to try it. I was feeling braver now so I put a paw in. The fleece felt very nice and when I plucked up the courage to climb into the basket and lie down, I actually liked it. Ever since then I've enjoyed curling up in it. It's just the right size for me to fit in.

My basket is a real basket, made of woven willow stalks, and is about forty years old. When I shift my weight, the basket creaks a bit but it doesn't bother me because it's just the natural sound of the willow moving.

I'm not the first dog to enjoy snuggling up in this basket. It originally belonged to a collie named Tessa, who was my mum's first dog. She was small, like I am, jet black like me, with a white front, and had the classic white Border collie stripe on her face.

Although she had a very happy life with my mum, the story of how she came to live with her is quite sad. When she was a small puppy, Tessa went to live with a couple who had a little boy. Everything went well until the child became ill with breathing difficulties a few months later. He had all kinds of tests and it was found that he had asthma.

As if that was not hard enough for him to cope with, the family was also told that it was an allergy to their dog's fur that had caused the illness. Although the little boy was very upset, he had to part with his dog.

His parents put a notice in the window of a local paper shop: "Good home wanted for six months old Border collie. Collar, lead and brush included." It was my mum who gave Tessa the new home she needed.

What neither of them ever dreamed then, was that she would live with my mum for the next eighteen and a half years. That's a long life for a dog. Cat's often reach nineteen but dogs don't.

My mum told me the oldest dog she ever met was when she and Tessa were visiting York and were out for a walk on the racecourse. There was another lady exercising an elderly German shepherd. She told my mum her dog was twenty one years old.

Tessa was a well-travelled collie and not just in the car. She had no fear of going on a bus. She used to go away on holiday with my mum and was quite comfortable with catching a train. In London, she had even travelled on the underground. Mum had to carry her up the escalators because they are dangerous for dogs' paws.

Tessa had been on holiday with mum to Blackpool where she went on the trams. Tessa loved the beach. She was a dog with boundless energy and on the sands she could run and run to her heart's content.

Once, she went on a long boat trip to the Isle of Man and while they were there she went on the mountain railway up to the top of Snafell. Another time she travelled by boat to Guernsey in the Channel Islands.

The voyage took all day. That boat had a special deck just for dogs. Each dog was provided with its own cage and their owners could go and sit with them and keep them company.

Tessa was a well-behaved dog who got on with people and other animals. She went to obedience classes, like I do. I bet she was top of the class.

There was a gap of several years after Tessa before my mum went to the rescue to look for another collie. The dog she chose had lost its home because something had happened to the person she belonged to. She had been a much loved family pet. She had been trained by her original owner and managed the transition to her new home without much difficulty.

Her name was Callie and she came to my mum when she was seven – the same as me. She was small like me but her coat was smokey grey. She had a white front but she didn't have the typical white collie stripe on her face, although you could see it faintly when she turned her head to the side. Callie was a confident dog and settled down quickly with my mum.

The old railway path that we use didn't exist then but there was another one some distance away that mum used to drive them to. At that time she had a folding bike that she could put in the car. She liked to ride along, with Callie running beside her. Railway paths are good for cycling because they're generally flat.

Another of their favourite walks was along the canal towpath. That was a shorter drive from home. Before they got out of the car, mum always made sure Callie was firmly on the lead.

When mum got Callie, she didn't know about one of her little habits. The first time they went to the canal, Callie took one look and dived straight in! As mum walked along the towpath, her dog was swimming alongside her! That wasn't a problem until the time came for Callie to get out of the water.

She was obedient – she came when she was called – but she came trailing masses of smelly, green waterweed that was sticking to her coat, and shook herself all over mum and everybody else nearby.

Mum made her run round and round the car park until she was dry enough to get in the car. Callie had to go straight in the bath as soon as they got home and the horrible stinky smell of pondweed lingered in the car for ages afterwards.

Callie was a real water baby. She couldn't pass a puddle without jumping in it. Tessa had always kept her feet dry – she even managed to chase about on the beach without stepping into the sea.

My mum used to call Tessa 'LMDP', short for Little Miss Dainty Paws. She hated to get her feet dirty. She would run about on the lawn and never put a toe in a flower bed. Callie couldn't have been more different. She loved mud, newly dug earth and dirty water.

One of the things she liked to roll in, which annoyed mum more than anything, was any place where a fox had been and left its scent. If you haven't smelled that smell, don't bother. It's horrible – a sharp, pungent smell and the only way to get it off a dog's fur is to wash it off. Callie used to get a bath every time she got fox on her. I bet she did it on purpose because she liked going in the bath. Mum spent a fortune on dog shampoo.

Callie was my mum's loving companion for seven years. You can see her picture on the back of all my mum's books and on her web site.

There are two framed photographs in our sitting room, one on either side of the mantelpiece. On the left, there is Tessa at the beach on the Isle of Man; on the right is Callie in our garden. When my mum chose my name, she combined their two names to make Cassie, which she gave to me.

So I think of those two much loved collies as my older sisters. Their home was here with my mum, just as mine is today. She loved them both and they, in turn, loved her. They shared many happy years with her and I am hoping that I will be able to do the same.

Chapter 11 – Proud Day

There's one thing about my mum that really puzzles me. Every morning I follow her into the bathroom and watch her take all her clothes off and get into a glass box and spray water all over herself. She seems to really enjoy it. Sometimes she starts singing. I leave then and go and get into my basket.

Later on, when we go out, if it's raining she puts on wellies and waterproofs and sometimes takes an umbrella to make sure she doesn't get a drop of rain on her.

So does she like getting wet, or doesn't she? It's things like this that dogs find quite hard to understand about people. The nice thing about my mum and me is that no matter how hard we find it to understand one another, we never stop trying.

I watch my mum to see what she's thinking. People give away a lot about what's on their mind through their face. People have many more facial expressions than animals. For instance, when they're happy, people smile with their face – dogs smile with their tail.

People have different shaped eyes from dogs. Most animals show only the coloured part of their eyes. Unless I turn my eyes to the extreme right or left, there is no white to be seen. People, however, have a lot of white showing in their eyes all the time and by watching closely dogs can tell a lot about a person's feelings and mood. I don't just mean if they're crying. Without being aware of it, people give away a lot through eye movements.

Over the many thousands of years that dogs have lived around people they've become expert at reading these signs. That's why we don't need to understand every word our owner says to know what their intention is. In fact, we do better in some ways because those eye movements and other facial expressions cannot lie, like words can.

There is a belief that all modern dogs are descended from wolves. I suppose it could be true. People say I look a bit like a fox because I've got a little pointed face and a bushy tail. Foxes are wild animals. So although I'm a collie, which is a thoroughly domesticated breed, maybe it's not unreasonable to think wolf, somewhere far back in my ancestry.

If it's true, I'd like to say thank you to those first wolves who thought it was a good idea to move in and make friends with people. You did all us dogs a favour.

People have experimented with keeping modern wolves as household pets and treating them like dogs. It works up to a point while they're little cubs, but as soon as they grow up, their wild instincts come to the fore. They can't be taught to behave with respect for people. All they are interested in is food and they will wreck the place to get it.

Hummm, perhaps I do recognise the odd stirrings of wolf mentality there. I confess I have been known to disgrace myself when there was something to eat at stake. Never mind if I've had a bowlful of dog food, I still go after anything else edible. I can't help myself. There was that episode with the piece of chicken that my mum was going to have for tea.

Mum was very good about it and said it was really her fault for leaving it where I could reach it. But I still shouldn't have put my paws up on the kitchen worktop, I know that. I do try to remember my manners but I don't always succeed.

It's one area where mum has got the message quicker than I have. Now she makes sure not to leave anything eatable where I can get at it.

I have a problem with food in the street, too. There always seem to be chips and bits of pizza and half-eaten sandwiches lying about on roads where we go. I find it difficult to ignore food that's within easy reach and mum always has to remind me to 'leave' when we walk by.

Let's face it, unless you're a Crufts obedience champion – and there's only one of those a year – you are going to make mistakes sometimes.

I try to be as obedient as I can and I had an opportunity to prove how much effort I've been putting in when the time came for the bronze obedience award at training class.

The week before we took the test we practised our exercises over and over again. I could do them all at home, but would I get them right on the night, with the stress of all the other dogs and people around?

Every time she sat down with her lunch or a cup of tea, my mum picked up the list of questions she would have to answer as her part of the test – oh, yes, I wasn't the only one who had to do well to pass!

There were sections about how to look after me, the signs that I may be ill, keeping me wormed and flea-proofed, making sure I wasn't a nuisance to other people, using poo bags. There were loads of questions and she wanted to be certain she could remember the right answers to them all.

She marked different parts of the paper with different coloured felt pens. It looked very pretty. I think it was supposed to help her remember the different questions.

My mum likes colours. She said, one day, that next time she gets a dog it's going to be a green one so that when it sheds its hair it doesn't show on the carpet. I haven't actually seen any green dogs, although I admit I haven't been to very many places, but I think it might be hard for my mum to find a green collie. On the whole, she may be better off settling for a black carpet.

When the day of the test came I got an extra special grooming. I've always loved being brushed and combed so that was very nice.

There was quite a tense atmosphere in the hall when we arrived. There was a buzz of talk and the dogs were greeting each other more noisily than usual. Our trainer asked us to get down to work as quickly as possible because we had a full programme to get through.

The pace she set was certainly brisk. We moved from working in a circle to lining up, group activity to individual task. Some of the dogs were totally focused and performed all their commands faultlessly. For the rest of us things didn't go quite so well.

I suffered from my usual problem of catching sight of Cherry and not being able to drag my eyes away from her. That didn't cause me a problem when we were working in groups but I had a bad moment when I had to do an individual task. I completely forgot what to do when my mum asked me to fetch my little lion toy and give it back to her. I simply couldn't remember what I was supposed to do, although we had practised in the afternoon at home and I had done it perfectly. But, of course, Cherry wasn't in our sitting room!

Mum got quite sharp with me and made me concentrate and then I remembered and did it right, just in time!

Between tests, Ruby, who was sitting next to me, kept nibbling at my tail. Usually I don't mind her doing something like that but I was trying to keep my mind on the next task and she was putting me off. I was quite grumpy with her because I was having such a hard job trying to keep my concentration.

It was a long evening. We ran over our usual time by twenty minutes and I know I wasn't the only dog who was feeling tired by the end. But it was all worth it when names were announced at the end and I learned that I had passed my bronze test.

My mum proudly carried our certificate home. It has both our names on it and I feel very glad about that because our success was down to teamwork. In fact, everything we do is teamwork. It's one of the best things about living with my mum.

Chapter 12 – The Future

I started my story by giving you a list of all my belongings. Those were the things my mum gave me when I first came to live with her.

I'm going to give you another list now. After six months in this happy home these are the things I now have that I didn't have before, and that mean more to me, even, than the things in my first list:
> freedom
> safety
> love and affection
> friends
> good behaviour

All rescue dogs go to their new home wanting to be good and hoping to be accepted for what they are.

If they are well treated and given time to adapt, they will learn how to live up to their new owner's expectations of them. With love and patience, even a dog with the most difficult history can turn into the perfect pet.

I've already adapted from barn dog to house dog, country dog to town dog, working dog to playing dog, herding failure to obedience success.

I want to repay my mum for all her love and trust in me by becoming the very, very best friend I can be to her. I haven't got all the way there yet, but I'm working on it.

Wish me luck!